Everything You Always Wanted to Know About Increasing Business*

*AND WERE AFRAID TO ASK

Explained by Robert J. Smith, MFA and His Forbes Articles

Foreword by

Wayne Tupuola, CEO & Chairman, Laser Photonics Corporation

Copyright

Limit of Liability Disclaimer: The information provided in this book is for informational purposes only and is not intended to be a source of direct consulting with respect to the material presented. The information and/or documents contained in this book do not constitute legal or financial advice and should never be used without first consulting a qualified advisor to determine which strategies may best fit your individual needs and be customized to your unique situation.

The publisher and the authors do not make any guarantee or other promise as to any results that may be obtained from using the content in this book. Meeting with a qualified advisor and conducting your own research and due diligence is always recommended. To the maximum extent permitted by law, the publisher and the authors disclaim any and all liability in the event any information, commentary, analysis, opinions, advice and/or recommendations contained in this book prove to be inaccurate, incomplete, unreliable, or result in any type of loss.

Content contained or made available through this book is not intended to constitute legal advice or financial advice, and no attorney-client relationship is formed through this published work.

Client Consulting Relationships

May Only Be Formed Through:

https://SmithProfits.com

SCAN ME

Book a No-Charge, No-Obligation Consultation at:

https://SmithProfits.com/Contact/

Earnings Disclaimer: All income examples in this book are examples. They are not intended to represent or guarantee that everyone will achieve the same results. It is understood that each individual's success will be determined by his or her desire, dedication, background, effort, and motivation to work. There is no guarantee the reader will duplicate any of the results stated here. The reader recognizes that any and all business endeavors have inherent risk of loss of capital.

No Agency Relationship: The opinions of each co-author do not necessarily constitute the opinions of Robert J. Smith, Robert J. Smith Productions, or Smith Profits. Co-author content does not in any way constitute an agency relationship between any co-author and of Robert J. Smith, Robert J. Smith Productions, or Smith Profits.

Everything You Always Wanted to Know About Increasing Business*

***And Were Afraid To Ask: Explained by Robert J. Smith, MFA and His Forbes Articles**

1st Edition: 2026

ASIN: B0GC7SNQHG

ISBN: (eBook) 978-1-965538-15-9

ISBN: (Amazon Paperback) 978-1-965538-16-6

ISBN: (Amazon Hardcover) 978-1-965538-17-3

ISBN: (Ingram Spark Paperback) 978-1-965538-18-0

ISBN: (Ingram Spark Hardcover) 978-1-965538-30-2

ISBN: (Smashwords) 978-1-965538-31-9

Book Layout © 2026, **Published by:** Smith Business Books and Amazon Publishing Center.

Table of Contents

"Learning is not attained by chance. It must be sought for with ardor and attended to with diligence."

-Abigail Adams

Acknowledgements

This book would not have been possible without the love and patience of my wonderful family.

Thank you; Paulette Meunier, Ronald Smith, Ashley Smith, Austin Smith, Sabrina Smith and Sharon Roznowski.

Foreword
by Wayne Tupuola

#1 Best Selling Co Author of
***INFLUENCE IN ACTION™* for CEOs**
CEO & Chairman, Laser Photonics Corporation

In every industry I've ever operated in, from defense and aerospace to industrial manufacturing and now laser photonics, one brutal fact never changes:

Nothing happens until something is sold.

Technology can be brilliant. Operations can be lean. Capital can be abundant. However, if sales, visibility, and credibility aren't there, the rest is just potential energy. That's why what you're holding is so important: it's not theory, it's a practical operating system for turning influence into results.

Robert J. Smith has done something unique here. He hasn't written "another sales book." He's built a bridge between classic storytelling, timeless Hollywood and television icons, and the most rigorously researched principles of influence and persuasion, and then translated all of that into concrete, repeatable actions any business can implement.

And I want to emphasize that word: repeatable.

As a CEO, you don't have time for vague inspiration. You need levers you can pull, systems you can install, and strategies that scale beyond your own personality.

That's exactly what this book delivers.

Why This Book Matters to CEOs and Leaders:

Robert has lived what he's teaching. His track record: #1 worldwide producer in multiple Fortune 100, 500 and 1000 financial institutions; record breaking performance at blue chip firms; top 1% rankings in the Internet Movie Database (IMDb); and a long string of #1 Best Selling books is not accidental. It's engineered.

What impressed me most when I first got to know Robert wasn't just his credentials; it was the way he integrates them:

He understands sales at the street level, one prospect at a time.

He understands branding and media at the national and global level.

He understands influence and persuasion at the scientific, evidence based level.

Then he packages all of that into systems that other people, your people, can actually use.

This book is the clearest expression of that I've

seen.

From "Hollywood" to Your P&L!

You'll notice early on that Robert structures each chapter around a classic film or TV property: The Ten Commandments, King Kong, Citizen Kane, Network, The Three Musketeers, Requiem for a Heavyweight, Somebody Up There Likes Me, The Magnificent Seven, Candid Camera, Jingle All the Way, Friendly Persuasion, and Mad Men.

That's not a gimmick. It's modeling.

Every one of those titles represents a proven, enduring masterclass in attention, emotion, and memory. Hollywood and Madison Avenue have spent billions learning how to:

Hook attention in seconds.

Tell stories people actually remember.

Make messages spread.

Shape perception of brands, products, and personalities.

Robert's genius is that he doesn't ask you to "appreciate" that; he shows you how to use it in your business:

Turning The Ten Commandments into a clear, actionable "sales code" for your team.

Turning King Kong into a framework for

proven and affordable, leveraged publicity.

Turning Citizen Kane into a winning playbook for becoming a modern "business hyphenate" without burning out.

Turning Network and the timeless classic The Three Musketeers into practical systems for LinkedIn, media, and IMDb dominance.

Turning the ageless boxing films, Requiem for a Heavyweight, and Somebody Up There Likes Me into complete strategies for taglines and slogans that actually move money.

Turning Candid Camera and "smile science" into brand assets that make people feel good about buying from you.

Turning Jingle All the Way into a case for why your brand needs a hook the market can't forget.

Turning Friendly Persuasion into a proven field manual for Cialdini's principles in real world selling

And finally, turning Mad Men into a modern, CEO level view of how to build demand, not just respond to it.

If you've ever wondered, "How do I take what the big players do—Fortune 100 brands, major agencies, studios—and scale it down so it actually works for my company?" this book is your answer.

***INFLUENCE IN ACTION™*, Not in Theory.**

As co-author of ***INFLUENCE IN ACTION™*** for CEOs, I've spent a lot of time with leaders who understand that influence is now a core executive competency, not a "soft skill."

Robert doesn't just reference Dr. Robert Cialdini's work; he's built his business on it. He's a founding member of the Cialdini Institute, and you'll see the seven principles: Authority, Reciprocity, Scarcity, Consistency, Liking, Social Proof, and Unity, woven through every chapter:

Authority in how you position yourself as the obvious expert.

Reciprocity in the way you provide real value before you ever ask for a sale.

Scarcity in how you communicate your capacity and time.

Consistency in your follow up, reviews, and media cadence.

Liking in your personal brand, your smile, and your story.

Social Proof in your media, testimonials, rankings, and client results.

Unity in the way you work with affinity groups and defined communities.

This is what separates "persuasion" from "pressure." Robert is unapologetically focused on ethical, evidence based influence. He's not teaching tricks; he's teaching systems that align with how people really decide to do business.

Why I Believe This Book Is Different:

I read a lot of business content. Most of it falls into one of three buckets:

1. Academic but impractical.
2. Motivational but shallow.
3. Tactical but disconnected from a broader strategy.

This book avoids all three traps.

It's grounded in research, and it's written by a producer who's actually carried a quota, met payroll, and competed in brutal markets.

It's energizing, and it always comes back to "Proven Actions to Take" at the end of every chapter.

It's tactical, and every tactic ladders up to a cohesive system: more authority, more visibility, more persuasive power, more sales.

If you implement even a portion of what's in these pages:

A tighter tagline.

A real publicity strategy.

A LinkedIn and IMDb presence that support your authority.

A jingle or visual identity that makes people feel good about choosing you.

A disciplined use of influence principles in your sales process, you will see changes in your pipeline, your pricing power, and your brand perception.

A Final Word to the Reader:

As a CEO, I measure everything by one standard:

Does this help us win; ethically, sustainably, and at scale?

Robert J. Smith has created a playbook that does exactly that. He's taken a lifetime of selling, advising, writing, producing, and teaching and distilled it into a resource you can hand to your leadership team and say:

"Let's install this."

My suggestion is simple:

Read Chapter One and immediately map his "Ten Commandments" to your current sales process.

Then pick the one area where you're weakest; publicity, networking, authority positioning, tagline clarity, or use of influence principles, and apply the corresponding chapter aggressively for 90 days.

Treat this book not as something you "finish," rather as something you deploy.

If you do, you won't just understand influence. You'll see it; in your calendar, in your close rates, in your revenue, and in the way the market begins to see you.

To your continued success and to putting influence into action in your business.

Wayne Tupuola
CEO & Chairman, Laser Photonics Corporation
Co Author, ***INFLUENCE IN ACTION™*** for CEOs

Prologue

When writing for Forbes, Entrepreneur, Inc., Fast Company or any other media outlet, in any capacity, the first thing that you realize is that editors will routinely hatchet your work, so that you readers miss out on way too much. The worst part is that your readers are sometimes forced to miss what is most important to them.

Hence, the necessity for this book. I'm here to provide you with what the late, great Paul Harvey termed, "the rest of the story."

It is only with "the rest of the story" that you may receive the maximum benefit of any work.

Here's to you and here's to your continued success!

"Dost thou love life? Then, do not squander time, for that is the stuff that life is made of."

-Benjamin Franklin

Chapter One: Ten Commandments for Increasing Sales

THE TEN COMMANDMENTS Movie Poster 1956

Problems that Businesses Face:

Let's face it. One of the biggest problems that all businesses face, is a less than optimal sales volume. This consists of a less than ideal number of sales and/or an inferior amount of the size of those sales.

As Henry Ford, Thomas Watson and many others have famously stated, *"Nothing Happens until something is sold."* As this has always bene the case, and always will be the case, let's use the wisdom of the ages to increase sales now, and keep increasing them.

Smith's Forbes Article:

In 1956, The Ten Commandments, starring Charlton Heston, made its film debut. In the film, Heston, who plays Moses, makes his demand to the Pharaoh: "Let my people go!"

While certainly different circumstances, working in the financial services industry for the past five decades has given me my own set of 10 commandments for increasing sales, and my rallying cry has become, "Let my sales flow!" Now, I want to share those commandments with you. The best part is that you won't have to wander through the desert for 40 years to benefit.

1. Thou shalt commit to storytelling.

The film's director Cecile B. DeMille is often credited with saying, "The greatest art in the world is the art of storytelling." You want to frame your discovery meeting in a way that prepares your prospect to buy, and you can do this with factual storytelling. Use storytelling in every one of these edicts.

2. Thou shalt invoke reciprocation.

Prepare your prospective clients to reciprocate when they receive benefits from you. We all know that when someone does something for us, our nature makes us want to do something nice for them in return.

3. Thou shalt establish that you are in demand and your time is scarce.

Before they meet with me, my prospects understand that my time is not only valuable, my time is limited. People sometimes have to wait weeks to see me, and they know that when they do see me, our time is limited because I always have another client or prospect coming in right behind them.

4. Thou shalt present your authority.

If you are not yet an expert in your field, you need to gain expertise as quickly as possible. When I was a young financial advisor in metro Detroit, I had trouble getting Ford, Chrysler and General Motors executives to schedule appointments with me.

They all had much more life experience than I had, and many of them had been handling their own finances longer than I had been alive. I asked my general agent how I could gain credibility with them. Fortunately, he gave me great advice: "Earn your Chartered Life Underwriter (CLU) and Chartered Financial Consultant designations. As soon as they understand that you know more about how money works than they ever will, they will meet with you, and they will listen to you."

I completed those 48-month programs in only 13 months and received a surprise letter of commendation from my CEO for completing them in record time. I didn't do so to smash the company record, though. I did so to gain the expertise necessary to get appointments and close sales to provide for my wife and newborn child.

5. Thou shalt prepare your prospect to provide steady referrals.

Make it easy for your clients to provide you with steady referrals by providing great service. I had a couple of snowbird clients who summered in Florida and wintered in Nantucket. They did better than provide referrals; they made appointments. I would fly to Nantucket on a Sunday night, and they would have my entire week laid out for me and their millionaire friends lined up to meet with me.

6. Thou shalt establish consistency.

Communicate with prospects at a minimum of

once per month, whether that be in-person, through telephone calls, reports, magazines or newsletters. If you are not communicating with your prospects and clients, someone else is.

7. Thou shalt be likable.

If your prospects do not like you, they will not buy from you. Likability breeds trust. According to Dale Carnegie, 71% of customers would "rather buy from a sales professional they completely trusted than one who gave them a lower price."

8. Thou shalt prove your concept.

Providing proof of concept is the fastest and most effective way to gain credibility with your prospect and instill faith in your product or service. Proving a concept is not only efficient and effective, but concept proof can also be accomplished inexpensively.

For example, the gym I work out at, Iron Bodyfit, is a French company with more than 150 franchises throughout Europe and around the world. However, when moving into the United States and Canada, the French company quickly discovered that potential investors and franchisees here in the States approach things differently. As a result, they did a detailed tracking of a test subject over a three-month period to gain proof of concept they could show investors.

9. Thou shalt prove that your concept works for many individuals.

Make certain to show your prospects your client success stories and provide them with testimonials. Show them third-party case studies whenever possible.

For example, the equipment that Iron Bodyfit uses is approved by the Food and Drug Administration here in America. And the equipment company enlisted the aid of The Mayo Clinic to develop a controlled study to support their hypothesis that physical training with whole-body electronic muscle stimulation is superior to conventional training alone in healthy subjects.

10. Thou shalt establish reviews, at least annually.

Keeping your clients informed can help cement your status as a trusted advisor, and client reviews are necessary to track client progress. For example, I always meet with my financial advisory clients at least annually to track their investment results, to see if their tax status has changed or if their protection needs have changed, etc. That way, we know that they are always on track to meet or exceed their goals. This final commandment can not only help you to gain more business, but it can also help you to gain more referrals as well.

Paramount invested more than $13

million (roughly $120 million today), so that Heston could part the Red Sea as Moses. That investment made "The Ten Commandments" the highest grossing film in 1956, with more than $93 million made worldwide. It was also nominated for seven Academy Awards, including Best Picture.

The good news is that you don't have to invest millions to increase sales in your business—just consider my 10 commandments for increased sales.

Proven Actions to Take:

Infuse each and every one of these proven principles of influence into your business to increase sales, as early as today. Implement these proven strategies and stick with them, each and every day to skyrocket sales for your business.

Pro tip: Write a #1 Best Selling Book to increase your authority to massively increase your sales.

The **Median Increase in Income** for **#1 Best Selling Authors** is ***$96,000.00 Annually.***

This doesn't come from book royalties. This **annual six-figure increase** for businesspeople who are above the median comes from back-end business sales. With a **#1 Best Selling Book**, business owners and professionals gain authority that leads prospects to them who are **pre-sold on doing business** with them.

There is another benefit for **#1 Best Selling**

Authors who also engage in public speaking. **The average increase in fees** for public speakers with **#1 Best Selling Books is 350%.**

E.g., If you charge **$1,000.00** for a breakout session now. You can instantly raise your fees to **$3,500.00** and of you charge **$10,000.00** for a keynote speech, you can easily move your fees to **$35,000.00** and corporations and conferences will gladly pay it to have a **#1 Best Selling Author onstage for their attendees.**

Forbes and Entrepreneur both charge $150,000.00 and they both demand two to three years of your time for your book's completion. Neither guarantees any #1 ranking authority.

By contrast, we get the job done for you at a fraction of the cost, and at a fraction of the time. We also guarantee a #1 Best Seller for you. If you can't rank at the top, and if you can't gain much needed authority for you and your business, why bother?

Bonus Pro Tip:

Here is a way to amplify your authority with a **#1 Best Seller.** This is an example of my first **#1.** I wrote a quick chapter in an anthology and it was through this first-hand experience where I was able to develop the use of this powerful influence amplifier.

After years of record-breaking performance in

financial services with Fortune 500 Companies and others, it was natural for me to specialize in this industry when severe spinal cord and other injuries temporarily took away my ability to walk, and the subsequent surgeries forced me away from my financial advisory business, and into consulting other financial advisory firms.

As every business owner should know his or her competition, I knew mine. I was fortunate in that one of my direct competitors released a sales book at the same time that we released ours. This screenshot is directly responsible for me closing 10 out of 10 financial advisory firms shortly after the success of ***SALES GENIUS #1***.

I asked every boutique investment firm owner, every life insurance agency owner, and every asset management firm owner the same closing question. "Who else are you considering for your mush needed sales consulting?"

And, just like Perry Mason, I knew the answer before I asked the question. The answer was always a variation of this same result. "It's down to you and The Wolf of Wall Street." Knowing that, my response was always this highly effective question, immediately after showing them this image. "Why would you pay twice the price only to settle for second best?"

I've got nothing against Mr. Belfort. In fact, I'm grateful for all the business that he isn't even aware that he assisted me in gaining.

My teams and I can help you do the same for your business and for your legacy. Here is a screenshot we are able to grab for a retired President of UPS International:

It's great to see our client at #**1** and his ideological opposition at #3. How would you like to rank #**1** and see your direct competition ranked at #2, #3, or not at all?

Book a No-Charge, No-Obligation Consultation to

Get Your #1 Best Selling Book Completed Here:

https://SmithProfits.com/Contact/

Chapter Two: Publicity, The Ninth Wonder Of The World

KING KONG Movie Poster 1933

Problems that Businesses Face:

- Lack of Brand Awareness
- Lack of Credibility
- Lack of Authority
- Lack of Budget to Accomplish these Absolute Necessities

Smith's Forbes Article:

King Kong was billed as "the eighth wonder of the world." Since that is the case, I think publicity must be the ninth wonder of the world.

The work of the Ringling Brothers, P.T. Barnum and Bailey Circus became widely known as the Greatest Show on Earth. This happened largely through the massive efforts of P. T. Barnum, who is believed to have famously stated, "Without publicity a terrible thing happens, nothing."

Business owners certainly don't want "nothing" to happen to their businesses. No one wants that. In fact, publicity is so important that Barnum is also believed to have started the common saying, "There is no such thing as bad publicity." While that may be argued, the fact is that when people are talking about your business, you have top-of-mind awareness with them.

Jane Russell is credited with saying, "Publicity

can be terrible. But only if you don't have any." If you don't have any publicity, you don't have top-of-mind awareness with your target customers. If you do have top-of-mind awareness, there isn't much "terrible" about that.

Publicity is a must-have for every business, large, small and in-between. The question is, as a business owner, how do you gain publicity? Fact is, you can gain it in several ways, all with little or no cost.

Make it easy for people to find you online.

For example, if you appear on television, in films and even on podcasts, you owe it to yourself to build your Internet Movie Database (IMDb) page. It works for my company, and it can work for you, too. We have booked a lot of film, television and commercial appearances simply by being seen and by being easily found online. We've added a host of new customers and clients as well. You can do the same.

In addition to an IMDb page, I recommend that all of our clients receive as much media attention as possible. One way is with the traditional press release in the hopes that their companies get picked up. I've found that a better way is to create stories yourself and distribute them to hundreds of media outlets, including the leading television networks.

Once that publicity has been obtained through television or radio appearances, digital or print stories, make certain that you let prospective and current clients or customers know about it. Deliver links to your interviews and stories to your audience. I've found this can enhance credibility, strengthen client relationships and lead to more referrals. These interview and story links may be added to email signatures, in email blasts, in client newsletters, placed on websites, added to YouTube and Vimeo channels, etc.

One thing that must be avoided is complacency. All of the publicity in the world won't do a business any good if everyone inside of it merely sits back and waits for the phone to ring. While it might ring, these calls are only the tip of the iceberg. Smart business leaders know that the bulk of success earned from publicity is earned below the surface. It's not enough to be in the media—our target audience, our customers and clients must know that we are in the media.

Just like personal trainers tell us in the gym, "Consistency is key!" Aim to be in the media with positive stories about your business on a consistent basis. It's not enough to make one single media splash and then rest on your laurels. Consistent business can be a predictable result when you are consistently seen as industry experts in front of your clients, prospects and others.

Look for podcast opportunities.

If mass media is not for you, simply consider a newer type of media: podcasts. You can appear with strategic partners or anyone who has questions that you are well-equipped to answer. There are hundreds, if not thousands of podcasters with audiences that have problems that you and your company can solve for them.

While I've been asked to be interviewed in all of the podcasts I've appeared on, it's not difficult to locate podcast opportunities. If you listen to podcasts on a regular basis, reach out directly to your favorite podcasters and see if they'd like to share your expertise with their audience. This method is certainly cost-effective if not an effective use of your time. If reaching out to podcasts directly isn't for you or if you simply don't have time for it, a competent PR specialist can certainly handle this for you.

Stand out.

In my experience, it has never been easier to have your business featured on major television news networks, and it has never been easier to find your way onto network affiliates to make live appearances. Still, many companies and business leaders fail to do so on a consistent basis.

As Bruce Serbin says, "Whether you are an author, entrepreneur or expert, being a regularly featured guest expert in the media is one of the biggest credibility builders for your brand. It's an implied endorsement that tells people you are smart, trustworthy and a true expert in your field. The perception is if the media turns to you for insights, you must know what you are talking about." (Disclosure: I've worked with Bruce Serbin over the years.)

We know that King Kong ended with the famous line, "It was beauty killed the beast." To keep your beast of a business alive and growing, harness the ninth wonder of the world. Get publicity now and get it often!

Proven Actions to Take:

Leverage affordable publicity to increase brand awareness, build credibility, build authority and do so within your budget. Only increasing your budget as new revenues from your publicity allow you to do so.

Follow the late great, Sam Walton's lead. We've adopted his winning philosophy, and you can, too!

https://SmithProfits.com

SCAN ME

No budget is too large, and no budget is too small. They key is to take ACTION and get started, now. You will see results from your very first effort, and you can reinvest in your company from there. Grow at your own pace, safe and secure, with only proven methods.

Book Your <u>Guaranteed</u> Television Interviews

and Publicity, Here:

https://SmithProfits.com/Contact

Chapter Three:
Citizen Hyphenate: Use Kane's Strategy to Increase Business

CITIZEN KANE Movie Poster 1941

Problems that Businesses Face:

Many businesspeople start out as the "Chief Cook and Bottle Washer." That was no problem for Orson Welles, it was no problem for me in making corporate training films, PSAs and shorts. It should be no problem for you, either.

While we can each do it all, the good news is that we don't have to. Here is the catch; while we don't have to do everything, we should know how to do everything so that we know when it is done well, by others. For example, in the Internet Movie Database (IMDb) where I am fortunate enough to join the late great, Orson Welles in the Top 1% of their rankings, you will never find me credited as a film editor. However, you will often find me credited as a supervising editor.

I am glad to have won a Director's Award for Editing for Film, Games, and Animation. Just the same, it is not efficient for me in my business to do the tedious work, myself. For maximum efficiency, I merely oversee specialists who do that work for me. You can do the same.

Smith's Forbes Article:

Orson Welles was a hyphenate. In other words, Mr. Welles routinely performed more than one job function at a time. For example, in what many consider to be the greatest film of all time, Citizen Kane, Mr. Welles served as writer-director-producer-actor. Although there has been much debate over whether the bulk of the script was written by Herman J. Mankiewicz, you get the point of the hyphens.

"Good evening, ladies and gentlemen," Mr. Welles once said, "My name is Orson Welles. I am an actor. I am a writer. I am a producer. I am a director. I am a magician. I appear on stage and on the radio. Why are there so many of me and so few of you?"

Having made scores of films as a writer, director, producer and actor myself, I can honestly say there are two differences between one of my heroes and fellow hyphenates, Mr. Welles and myself. Those two things are both fame and fortune.

So, what does this have to do with business? A lot. For one thing, Mr. Welles made a very handsome living as a hyphenate while he put many people to work. How about you? Have you ever considered yourself as one of us, even unknowingly? Have you ever referred to yourself as "chief cook and bottlewasher?" If you have, then you, my friend, are also a hyphenate.

There are more of us than one might think for the simple reason: As the saying goes, a business owner must wear many hats. At any given time, an owner works as a manager, an accountant, a sales trainer, a customer service representative and at a host of other jobs.

While there are times a business owner must step into various roles, the company benefits most when its leader spends as much time as possible in productive activities. Of course, writing, directing, producing and acting are just as essential in business as they are in the film industry.

Show business is like any other business.

Welles on writing: "I know that, in theory, the word is secondary in cinema, but the secret of my work is that everything is based on the word. I always begin with the dialogue."

The success of all businesses largely depends on the written word. Written business plans, marketing plans, mission statements and sales scripts are essential to the success of any business.

Welles on directing: "My kind of director is an actor-director who writes."

A director fully immersed in all major aspects of production is optimal. The bottom line is that leadership is crucial to any business. From the creation of the company's vision to seeing that all directives are carried out, one person and only one person must take ultimate responsibility.

Welles on production: “I look back on my life and it’s 95 percent running around trying to raise money to make movies and five percent actually making them.”

The work necessary to capitalize on one’s company might not provide the same intrinsic rewards as the production of one’s product or service. Nevertheless, capitalization is necessary. Once that necessity has been accomplished, sales and other teams must produce at optimal efficiency.

Welles on acting: President Franklin D. Roosevelt once told Welles, "You and I are the two best actors in America."

Business owners become actors every time they give a speech, every time they attempt to persuade and, quite literally, every time they are featured in a television commercial for their business. A perfect example is one of America’s most prolific pitchmen for his own business, attorney John Morgan, founder of Morgan and Morgan. The chairman of the largest personal injury law firm in the United States is also featured in my upcoming book about becoming No. 1.

Actor Joseph Cotton said, “Orson Welles lists Citizen Kane as his best film, Alfred Hitchcock opts for Shadow of a Doubt, and Sir Carol Reed chose The Third Man – and I’m in all of them.”

I know how that great actor felt when he made

that statement. While it might not be modest, it is rewarding to know that you've contributed to the great works of modern masters at great companies. For Cotten, it was with Welles at RKO, Hitchcock at Universal Pictures and Reed (also again with Welles) at StudioCanal (France).

For me, it was reaching No. 1 in production out of thousands of agents with Mutual of New York/AXA, setting records at John Hancock and being part of a great New York Life team that was recognized for 50 consecutive years of leadership in the Million Dollar Round Table. While it's no star on the Hollywood Walk of Fame, it is an honor to have my name on a plaque in the lobby of the New York Life Building on Madison Avenue with all of the others who contributed to reaching that milestone.

What is your masterpiece?

Many consider one of my less commercially successful comic books to be my masterpiece. The reason is that I've used that specific work to volunteer to teach elementary school students the art of writing for years. Although I've had more commercially successful works to date, one cannot put a price on teaching America's youth an indispensable skill. Either way, I'm not satisfied as of yet. I'll reproduce each of those works in other forms of media. I'll keep creating other works as well.

How about you? Is your current business your masterpiece? Is a former business your best work? Was your masterpiece something else that you created? Is it something new that you are working on now?

Take an inventory of the roles that you play in your business. Are you a copywriter-sales producer-marketing director-television commercial actor? If your inventory looks anything like this, you are also a hyphenate.

Proven Actions to Take:

No matter what you do, be the very best you can be at it. Hire trained people to do the work they can do and orchestrate your entire productions so that each one will be the very best that you and your team can make it.

Book a No-Charge, No-Obligation Consultation to Create Your

Marketing Strategy to Increase Sales, Revenues, and Profits:

https://SmithProfits.com/Contact/

Chapter Four: Network Like Your Business Depends On It

Your Author, Kevin Harrington from ABC's Shark Tank, Your Author's Mother, Paulette Meunier

Problems that Businesses Face:

- Lack of a networking strategy
- Lack of results from networking
- Lack of public speaking opportunities
- Lack of success with public speaking

Smith's Forbes Article:

The logline for the 1976 movie "Network," is "A television network cynically exploits a deranged former anchor's ravings and revelations about the news media for its own profit but finds that his message may be difficult to control."

While Howard Beale (played by Peter Finch) may have been deranged and had no control over his network, you are competent and may carry out proven strategies to control your networking efforts for optimal results. Here's how:

Gain credibility through LinkedIn.

LinkedIn has nearly a billion members, spread across 200 countries but with the largest contingent living in the United States. However, what most executives don't know is that the site contains a useful tool that helps members keep score and improve their efforts called "Your Social Selling Index" or SSI.

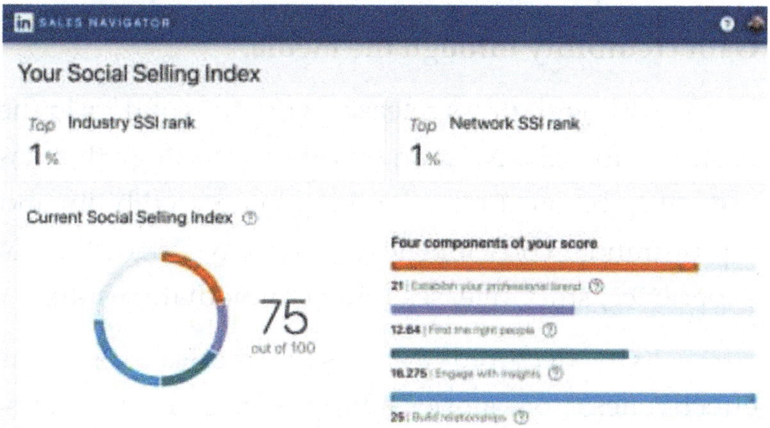

The tool tracks individual member rankings by industry and by network. As of this writing, my LinkedIn SSI ranks me in the top 1% of my industry and the top 1% of my network. For me, combining SSI improvements with a broader strategy has proven to be most effective. And I've seen firsthand how leveraging LinkedIn networking efforts with media appearances and rankings in the Internet Movie Database (IMDb) has worked time and again for other executives and business owners.

Improving your rankings can greatly improve your visibility and credibility, especially when you're reaching out to new people on LinkedIn. Most professionals see the value in "networking up" to reach key decision-makers who have the ability to quickly act on business offerings, as it's always more effective and more efficient to prospect companies from the top down than from the bottom up.

Gain credibility through the media.

Although press releases worked wonders in the past, I've found a twist on this classic strategy that has proven to be most effective in gaining credibility and top-of-mind consciousness. In my decades of experience, story releases return immediate results.

I've lectured across America on the effectiveness of stories. Storytelling is the First Commandment in my first Forbes article, "Ten Commandments for Increasing Sales." A well-written story release can be picked up by major network television affiliates and add credibility and authority to your work (my Fourth Commandment). Story releases may also be linked to clients in newsletters, email signatures and other sales and marketing efforts for predictable success. This is a strategy that my clients use on a daily basis. When I meet with our clients to review their progress (my Tenth Commandment), I am always pleased to hear them tell me about the new clients and new business they gained as a direct result of these efforts.

Gain credibility through IMDb.

Although most executives are aware of IMDb, they mistakenly believe that the Amazon-owned site and its rankings are reserved only for those celebrities we see on TV and in the movies—people like Peter Finch, Faye Dunaway and William Holden, who appeared in "Network" and have been stars for decades. But IMDb is not just for movie stars and their fans. In fact, IMDb is a "fan-tastic" site for business executives to gain credibility, notoriety and even some celebrity status in the minds of their clients and prospects.

I originally set my page up for film appearances and television interviews. Of course, not everyone is asked to be on live TV. However, you can also qualify for an IMDb listing if you've appeared on a podcast—this is true whether they are audio/video or audio only.

From a pure business point of view, IMDb can

also be a great equalizer when it comes to achieving front-page Google search rankings and even No. 1 Google search rankings. How else would this writer be able to consistently outrank an NFL running back and a rockstar who both have the same names? How else would this writer be able to consistently outrank in excess of 409 million listings of one of the most popular (as opposed to common) names in American history, Robert Smith?

Where do you personally rank when you Google search your own name? This ranking depends on a number of factors such as the uniqueness of your name and how you market your personal, professional and business brands. If your name is unique, you will simply not have to compete as hard for prospects and clients to be able to find you.

That said, if you have a more common name, there are things you can do to improve your ranking. For example, I've worked with Andrew Barrett, CEO of a securities firm. He initially didn't rank on the first page of Google, but adding his middle initial "Q" helps him rank at the top when people search for him as Andrew Q. Barrett.

My rockstar counterpart is the lead singer from The Cure and markets himself simply as Robert Smith. His marketing efforts ignore his middle name of James. In doing so, he always bests both the former Vikings running back—whose middle name is Scott—and myself, with the middle name of John. Here is where it gets interesting.

My IMDb listing includes my middle initial. The reason is that when I compete for local and national television commercial acting roles in Florida, there are four other actors here named Robert Smith. There were times when I would drive across the state for a role I was cast in, only to find one or two of the other actors with my name there as well.

My middle initial immediately became a difference-maker. Once I added it to my IMDb profile (and my business sites), I never again had to contend with my namesake. IMDb carries over 500 million listings, including nearly 13 million name listings that are ranked on a weekly basis. As such, my consistent work (my Sixth Commandment) has allowed me to repeatedly rank in the top 1% on IMDb. That ranking has also allowed me to consistently rank in the top 1% of Google searches and, most often, at the very top.

If a business hyphenate who grew up as a blue-collar worker in metro Detroit and became a white-collar worker in metro Orlando can do it, you certainly can! Simply give these proven strategies a try.

Proven Actions to Take:

- Create a networking strategy – Regularly schedule local and virtual networking events.

- Build results from networking – Strategy and Consistency Are Key. Stick with the events that bring results. Ditch the rest. They are merely time wasters.
- Create public speaking opportunities – Your #1 Best Selling Book Will Create More Opportunities Than You Ever Imagined.
- Build success with public speaking – Remember that Your #1 Best Selling Book Will Also Support Increasing Your Fees 400%, Like I Increased Mine.

Book a No-Charge, No-Obligation Consultation to

Build Your Networking Strategy and Create Speaking Opportunities:

https://SmithProfits.com/Contact/

Chapter Five:
The Three Marketing Musketeers

THE THREE MUSKETEERS **Movie Poster 1948**

Problems that Businesses Face:

- Lack of a Clear Marketing Strategy
- Lack of Authority on LinkedIn
- Lack of Media Presence
- Lack of Any Presence on IMDb to Support Top of Google Search Rankings

Smith's Forbes Article:

In the 1948 film The Three Musketeers, starring Lana Turner, Gene Kelly, Van Heflin and Vincent Price, the IMDb Logline reads, "D'Artagnan and his Musketeer comrades thwart the plans of Cardinal Richelieu to usurp King Louis XIII's power." Lucky for us, we don't have to thwart a political uprising with brilliant swordplay. We merely have to beat our competition with proven marketing. Thankfully, just like D'Artagnan, we have three musketeers by our side. Those three marketing musketeers are LinkedIn, the media and the Internet Movie Database (IMDb).

Those three marketing musketeers are the very same three that helped us improve our networking efforts in my previous article, "Network Like Your Business Depends On It." Now that we've improved your networking efforts, let's leverage those gains. By definition, let's use those newfound gains to your maximum advantage.

Leverage your upgraded LinkedIn credibility.

How much have you already been able to increase your LinkedIn Social Selling Index since reading my most recent article? Where do you rank in your industry and network now?

Your upgraded credibility on LinkedIn will help you make more and better connections. As stated in my previous article, my LinkedIn SSI ranks me in the top 1% of my industry and network. Yes, I've worked to maintain those rankings with media additions to my profile. It's never enough for your marketing efforts to reach optimal performance; your marketing efforts have to stay optimized.

With a polished profile, I've been able to make many gains recently, such as locating a quality graphic arts team, for which I had been searching for quite some time; received a book publishing offer; received quality referrals for my company's services and more. While that may look like luck, I've found that the harder we work, the luckier we get.

Hopefully, you've seen vast improvements in both your industry and network rankings by improving your profile through the media that you've been featured in over the past month. If your media relations were handled properly, you've gained visibility in all major TV networks through hundreds of affiliates from coast to coast and border to border. Hopefully, you've completed at least one live television interview or podcast over the past month and featured it in your LinkedIn profile as well.

If you haven't seen vast improvements in your SSI, here's how you can improve your profile to quickly make those gains:

1. Your LinkedIn profile serves as your landing page for potential connections. Make sure it closely reflects your brand.
2. Your name should reflect any professional designations or academic degrees you would like featured (e.g., MBA for business analysis or MFA for creative work).
3. Make certain that your images are clear and use them to give your audience some insight into you at work.
4. Use your company slogan as your headline if you have one. If not, simply create a compelling headline that lets readers know what to expect from you and your business.
5. Rather than "YourCompany.com," consider a hyperlink to your site that gives prospective clients a reason to visit (e.g., "Increase profits with Smith!" with a link directly to your site).
6. Create a custom LinkedIn URL. Detailed instructions are found on that site.
7. List publications, projects, volunteer work, etc.
8. If you haven't yet received any recommendations, provide them to others.

You'll be pleasantly surprised how well the law of reciprocity will work for you.

Leverage your upgraded media credibility.

As our company website states, "Profit begins with PR!" I don't recommend that anyone discontinues their business advertising. Our advertising did very well for us when we wanted to get off to a fast start. Now, however, we rarely advertise our services. There are four reasons for this:

1. We've created systems that provide us with a steady stream of never-ending referrals. If your business provides products and services that exceed customer and client expectations, you should be able to do the same. I certainly hope that you do.
2. We leverage our media credibility with every one of our hard-earned referrals, and you can do the same with yours.
3. Our public relations efforts have virtually eliminated our need to advertise. In fact, I'm hard-pressed to remember the last time that we ran any advertising.
4. We leverage our media credibility to earn even more media appearances for ourselves and for our clients. You will find this to be the case for both you and your business if you haven't already.

Leverage your upgraded IMDb credibility.

In "Network Like Your Business Depends On It," I shared the fact that your podcasts, television and film appearances (more on how business executives may acquire these in a future article) can qualify you for your very own IMDb profile, which will add to your credibility. I've picked up plenty of business as a direct result of my IMDb profile. Hopefully, you have as well. If you haven't set your profile up yet, what are you waiting for? Your competition won't create it for you.

As you learned last month, professionally created and well-written IMDb profiles can help improve Google search rankings and positioning. Hopefully, your IMDb profile has already earned you and your business No. 1 Google search rankings. If your listings have not reached No. 1 yet, you can work toward those rankings. Hopefully, you have at least reached the coveted "front page" of Google searches.

We all know that the majority of people who Google search products and services never leave the front page. In fact, the majority of people never leave the top of the front page. That's where all the click-throughs are. Human behavior dictates that most people will never take the time to even look past the first few results. As an example, how often do you scroll down to the bottom of the front page? How often do you look past the front page — if ever?

Put these three marketing musketeers to work for you in your business. Watch your customer/client base, your sales, your revenues and your profits grow as a direct result. Cardinal Richelieu never had a chance against The Three Musketeers. Your competition won't stand a chance against you, your business and the three marketing musketeers either. As Alexandre Dumas penned, "All for one and one for all!"

Proven Actions to Take:

- Develop a Clear Marketing Strategy, Either on Your Own, or Hire Us to Develop a Custom Marketing Strategy for You.
- Build Your Authority on LinkedIn or Hire Us to Guide You Through It.
- Lack of Media Presence. Start Doing Television and Other Media Interviews, Now. Don't Know Where to Start? We GUARANTEE Television Appearances and Print Media Placements for You.
- Lack of Any Presence on IMDb to Support Top of Google Search Rankings. We Can Build an Effective IMDb Presence for You and Greatly Improve Your Google Search Rankings, Even if You Don't Think You Qualify.

Book a No-Charge, No-Obligation Consultation

to Create a Clear Marketing Strategy,

Dominate on LinkedIn,

Create a Media Presence, and

Dominate Google Searches:

https://SmithProfits.com/Contact/

Chapter Six:
Requiem For A Heavyweight Tagline: How To Create One For Your Business

REQUIEM FOR A HEAVYWEIGHT **Movie Poster 1962**

Problems that Businesses Face:

- They Lack a Memorable Tagline
- They Fail To Consistently Employ a Memorable Tagline in Their Marketing and Advertising

Smith's Forbes Article:

Most people are unaware that one of television's most influential and prolific writers, Rod Serling, the creator of "The Twilight Zone," also wrote influential films such as "Patterns," "Seven Days in May," "Planet of the Apes" and "Requiem for a Heavyweight." The IMDb logline for the latter film is "Knockout performances by Anthony Quinn, Jackie Gleason, Mickey Rooney and Julie Harris highlight this hard-hitting drama of corruption in the ring." The 1962 movie also had many taglines, including:

- The World of "Mountain" Riviera...The Fast Buck...The Angry Men...The Lonely Women!
- The Gutsiest Picture Ever Made!
- They beat him...they broke him...they betrayed him...but they could not crush the towering dignity of a real fighter!

Of course, a requiem is a memorial, a remembrance of something that is no more. One of the greatest advertising tactics in the history of business—taglines—is something that has been forgotten by many of today's businesses, especially smaller businesses. I believe forgetting business taglines and campaign slogans can be a major mistake.

Well-Known Business Taglines

One of the world's most iconic brands, Coca-Cola, has had nearly 50 taglines to date. Being a home market merchandiser, a.k.a. route truck delivery driver for Coke in my youth, my personal favorites are "It's the Real Thing" "Coke is It!" and "The Pause That Refreshes" Of course, there are other taglines that businesses have scored knockouts with, including:

- I Can't Believe I Ate the Whole Thing (Alka Seltzer)
- It's not easy bein' cheesy (Cheetos)
- When it absolutely, positively has to be there overnight. (FedEx)
- Leave the Driving to Us (Greyhound)
- When You Care Enough to Send the Very Best (Hallmark)
- It Takes a Licking and Keeps on Ticking (Timex)
- Save Money. Live Better. (Walmart)

As you can see from these examples, the most effective taglines are catchy and memorable. What is the tagline for your business? Do you have one? If not, there is no time like the present.

Creating Your Business Tagline

When I wrote the screenplay, "Everything is

Temporary"(which eventually became "The Junior Partner") I had my protagonist, Champ Mitchell speak the phrase, "Everything is Temporary," and it made me wonder what name had been given to that literary device. As I completed my Creative Writing Master of Fine Arts at Full Sail University simultaneously with my Feature Film Writing degree program at UCLA, I asked every professor at each college. I was shocked to discover that no one had ever given a name to it. So, I took it upon myself to do so.

I run all of my taglines, slogans and ad copy by my co-producer and screenplay editor, Sharon Roznowski. She helped me coin the term “title punch” to describe when a movie title is spoken or otherwise shown in a film. Further research shows that our instincts to coin the term "title punch" were on the nose. Tagline, as defined by Merriam-Webster, is "a reiterated phrase identified with an individual, group or product." Slogan, on the other hand, is "a final line (as in a play or joke), especially one that serves to clarify a point or create a dramatic effect."

The title punch at the end of the Edmond O'Brien 1949 classic "D.O.A." did exactly that as it clarified the theme, title and point of the entire film with the final words spoken by actor Roy Engel. After a deputy asked him, “How shall I make out the report on him, captain?” Engel's character, a homicide detective, replies, "Better make it 'dead on arrival.'"

Director Rudolph Maté even gave it the one-two title punch when he followed those last words with a visual of a hand stamping the letters D.O.A. onto the police report.

The primary reason that I added the word "punch" to the title when any one of a number of other words would do is that I felt that when you hear or see the title of a movie in a movie, it should have significance. It should feel as if it hit you right in the face. A great business tagline should do the same! It should let your customers know what you can do for them, and it should stake your claim to your market share. Your tagline should be bold.

At my company, our tagline is "Hammering Out Profits for Your Business." Our tagline was easy to come up with as a blacksmith or "smithy" is our mascot across all of our brands and appears in all of our logos. Another example: When we formed Robert J. Smith Productions, we came up with the tagline, "Have a Productive Day!" We use it in all forms of communication that we have with our clients, vendors and strategic partners, and it's amazing how many referrals we receive simply because our e-mail signatures close with our tagline. The same strategy can work for your company as well. To create effective taglines, simply develop short statements that fit with your company's core products and services. Also, think about statements that blend well with your logos and other images. Then, use it everywhere. Once you've developed an optimal tagline for your business, you are also halfway to creating an effective jingle for use on your website and in radio and television commercials.

I'll leave you with two taglines from professional boxers who went into business for themselves after they retired from the ring: In promoting his fitness program, "Lightning" Lloyd Ellett borrows a popular saying among United States Navy Seals: "Slow is smooth. Smooth is fast." In selling the George Foreman Grill, "Big" George Foreman said, "It's so good I put my name on it!"

Whether you hire a PR firm or any advertising agency or you simply brainstorm with your associates, family, or friends, I think you'll see your business improve with a great tagline. You don't have to be Anthony Quinn, Jackie Gleason, Mickey Rooney or Julie Harris to create a "knockout performance." You don't have to be Rod Serling to create a heavyweight tagline. In the words of Nike: "Just Do It!"

Proven Actions to Take:

- Create a Memorable Tagline or Have Us Do It for You.
- Consistently Employ Your Memorable Tagline in Your Marketing and Advertising. Use it in Every Social Media Post and in Every

Television, Newspaper and Magazine Interview You Do.

Book a No-Charge, No-Obligation Consultation to

Create Memorable Taglines that Earn Massive Amounts of Business:

https://SmithProfits.com/Contact/

Chapter Seven:
'Somebody Up There Likes Me' And My Business: A Lesson On Taglines

SOMEBODY UP THERE LIKES ME **Movie Poster**
1956

Problems that Businesses Face:

- They Lack More Than One Memorable Tagline
- They Lack Memorable Slogans
- They Fail to Use Their Taglines and Slogans Consistently

Unclear about the differences between taglines and slogans? Here they are: A tagline is a permanent, high-level brand phrase that represents your company's overall identity. By contrast, a slogan is a temporary, phrase that is specific to an individual product or service that is used in specific marketing campaigns.

Smith's Forbes Article:

The IMDb logline for Somebody Up There Likes Me, starring Paul Newman, Pier Angeli and one of my all-time favorites Everett Sloane is, "Boxer Rocky Graziano's biopic, based on his autobiography, from childhood to his World Middleweight Championship title win at age 28 in 1947."

It's nice to see what life may have been like in the year both of my parents were born. The year 1947 was the beginning of the baby boom. Post-World War II, America was indeed the land of opportunity.

The film's tagline, "A girl can lift a fellow to the

skies," may have inspired its star with an eventual tagline for Newman's Own Pizza and the Newman's Own Foundation. Both carry what I consider to be one of the best taglines of all: "100% profits to help kids."

Tough Times

The years leading up to 1947 were another story. Rocky Graziano, whose real name was Thomas Rocco Barbella, was often in trouble with the law. Rocco, as he was originally known, was in and out of reform school, jail and prison.

The middleweight, who initially fought under his real name of Barbella, reportedly punched an officer and went AWOL from the U.S. Army. At the same time, my grandfather, Robert J. Smith Sr., only punched officers in the ring and became the U.S. Army Air Force Middleweight Boxing Champion. Barbella eventually began using the name Graziano when he fought. In Somebody Up There Likes Me, Rocky tells his eventual trainer that his last name is Graziano, "like the Italian wine." However, I've seen some accounts claim that he simply took his grandfather's last name, while others say he took the last name of his sister's boyfriend.

Ah, the magic of movies. As for the Graziano Family of Wines, they market their business by saying, "Our wines reflect an artistic blend of our Italian heritage with a touch of California flair." As far as business after boxing, the story goes that Graziano opened a restaurant when he retired from the ring. That New York restaurant was named Rocky Graziano's Pizza Ring. I haven't found the taglines that Rocky used to turn that restaurant into a successful franchise.

Tough Fighters

In my last article, "Requiem for a Heavyweight Tagline," I covered the business taglines of two other retired professional boxers, George Foreman and Lloyd Ellett. Here are additional phrases that each of these fighters and businessmen have used:

- George Foreman's grill: "Knock out the fat!"
- Lloyd Ellett's Fight Shape Project: "Helping Executives Perform Like A Champion."

Have you come up with a proven tagline for your business yet? If not, spar with Rocky and come up with one for Rocky Graziano's Pizza Ring. From there, you'll gain the experience to develop a new tagline for your business.

Here are some tips for creating effective taglines:

1. Differentiate your company from the competition. Don't sound like everyone else. Stand out from the crowd.
2. Keep it short. War and Peace is for the library,

not for your packaging, website or advertisements. Aim for six words or less. "Think" – IBM.

3. Make it memorable. The more your customers see your tagline, the more likely they are to remember it. Affix your tagline to your logo on your website and in all of your marketing and packaging materials.

   By contrast, learn from these mistakes:

- Dr. Pepper Ten: The "It's Not for Women" campaign alienated more than half of the population.
- AM/PM: "Imagine More Snacks Than You Can Imagine" must have come from the "Department of Redundancy Department."

Tough Taglines

Of course, the purpose of your tagline is to influence customers to buy your products and services. Effective business taglines are not well suited to influence political or cultural views. Effective business taglines are at their best when they influence consumer behavior. The more effective the tagline, the more the tagline influences consumer purchases, the higher the sales, revenues and profits.

Influence is a topic that we will cover in great detail in future articles. For now, let's consider Rocky Graziano's influence on acting as well as boxing and business. When preparing for the role of Stanley Kowalski, the washed-up boxer in A Streetcar Named Desire, the great Marlon Brando based his portrayal on Rocky Graziano. In fact, it's been said that Brando went to Rocky's gym to study him. Of course, Graziano paid no attention to the young actor. However, Brando gave Rocky two tickets to the film premiere, and when Rocky saw the film, he's known to have said, "The curtain went up, and on the stage is that son of a bitch from the gym, and he's playing me."

Another Brando and Malden film, One-Eyed Jacks, was partially written by Rod Serling, writer of Requiem for a Heavyweight. Of course, these days, Brando is the actor many believe to be the all-time greatest. As for Malden, he was as famous as a pitchman for American Express as he was for his 63 films. "American Express Traveler's Cheques—don't leave home without them." As traveler's cheques went out of style, that famous tagline evolved into a tagline for the AmEx credit card with many spokespeople promoting the tagline, "American Express, don't leave home without it."

Title Punch

If you've seen the film Somebody Up There Likes Me, you know that the title punch, which you learned about in my "Requiem" article, is spoken at the end of the movie. As Rocky and his wife, Norma, wave to adoring fans in a ticker-tape parade for the new world champion, screenwriters Ernest Lehman, Rowland Barber and Rocky Graziano himself have Paul Newman and Pier Angeli speak this dialogue:

Rocky: "You know, I've been lucky. Somebody up there likes me."

Norma: "Somebody down here, too."

There you have it. Get your business publicized, create a memorable tagline and somebody up there will like you, too. Do both the right way, and your customers and clients will like your business as well. Do both well and you and your business will be champions in your industry.

Proven Actions to Take:

- Create More Than One Memorable Tagline.
- Create Memorable Slogans.
- Use Your Taglines and Slogans Consistently to Drive New Business.

If you need help in creating effective taglines, slogans and marketing campaigns, we are here for you.

Book a No-Charge, No-Obligation Consultation to

Create Taglines and Slogans that Become Money-Making Machines:

https://SmithProfits.com/Contact/

Chapter Eight: 'The Magnificent Seven' Game Changers In Business

THE MAGNIFICENT SEVEN Movie Poster 1960

Problems that Businesses Face:

- They Lack Necessary Visibility
- They Lack Necessary Authority and Credibility
- They Foolishly Limit Themselves in Their Marketing and Advertising Mediums
- They Lack an Understanding of the Proven Principles of Influence and Persuasion
- Most Importantly, They Lack the Sound Advice of Professionals Who Have Attained the Great Achievements That They Strive For

Smith's Forbes Article:

The Internet Movie Database (IMDb) logline for the star-studded 1960 movie The Magnificent Seven is, "Seven gunfighters are hired by Mexican peasants to liberate their village from oppressive bandits." Thankfully, as a business owner, no one can call you a "peasant," and all you have to deal with is your competition. Here are seven game-changing strategies to help you do just that. Incorporate all seven, and your competitors don't stand a chance.

The taglines created for this film fit these seven game changers for business:

"Once You've Met Them...You'll Never Forget Them."

They Were Seven—They Fought like Seven

Hundred!"

In a word, these seven business strategies are "magnificent."

1. Television Network Placement

Instead of creating old-fashioned press releases in the hopes that some reporter somewhere will interview you for a story, why not hire a firm to create a story for you? Look for accomplished writers who can create stories for you and distribute them for placement by major television networks, in major magazines and other media outlets. Doing so can establish instant credibility for you and your business.

2. Leverage IMDb And The Media

Have you and/or your company been featured on television programs, film documentaries or podcasts? If so, you qualify for a profile in IMDb, an Amazon Company. Creating an IMDb profile can be a fast and economical way for both you and your business to rank on the front page of Google. You could rank in the number-one spot if you do it right. We've been creating IMDb profiles for decades, and we've seen this cost-effective strategy work time and time again.

3. Leverage Magazine Features And Cover Stories

Seeing you featured in magazines helps your clients and customers take pride in their decision to do business with you and your company. Seeing you on a magazine cover can make them eager to refer business to you. Case in point: I sent a magazine to clients that provided a wealth of information on topics that interested them. Two days after they were mailed out, I received a call from a client right from her mailbox. She was with a friend who wanted an introduction "to the man on the cover." That referred client hired us on our first visit and paid us an annual consulting fee. On our second visit, she made a million-dollar purchase.

4. Employ The Comic Book Marvel

Comics are more visually appealing than plain text. Comics capture attention and stimulate the imagination. More importantly, comics sell. We found ourselves in competition with six major financial firms, each with a team of advisors, CPAs and lawyers. Each company employed the traditional method of trying to make the sale with complex reports ranging from 50–200 pages in length. Of course, a confused mind always says "no."

We saw this as an opportunity to simplify matters for this elderly couple who just wanted their tax and liquidity problems solved. I created a comic book outline and created a superhero story to illustrate the key points and make very complex issues easy to understand. The couple immediately understood the concepts and made their decision to go with us on the spot. Our net revenues from that case were in excess of six figures. Thank you, comics.

The successful characteristics of a business comic have been proven to us for the past two decades. Simply follow the same successful storytelling methods that have proven successful since the beginning of time. First, stories must be entertaining to gain the interest of your audience. Second, stories must be coherent. They must follow the same three-act story structure that was handed down to us by the Ancient Greeks. Put simply, your business story must have a cogent beginning, middle and end. Third, your stories must be persuasive. Stories must include proven methods to influence your readers, audience, clients or customers.

5. Arrange Live Television Appearances

While appearing on local and national network television may not be for everyone, appearances can greatly benefit every business owner and professional. When you work with the right firms, you have the ability to cost-effectively book television interviews to bring your products and services in front of millions of buyers.

Television shows are often also glad to receive reciprocal publicity from you by providing you with professionally edited clips of your appearances for placement on your websites for life. This also enhances your credibility and authority with every visitor to your site.

6. Master The Principles Of Influence And Persuasion

If you want to gain more customers, close more sales and close more high-ticket sales, learn to be a master of influence and persuasion. Study research and methods developed by professionals. Study statistics. Numbers don't lie.

7. Consult Advisors

Hire someone who's been there before: someone who has reached levels of sales, revenues and profits that you and your company strive for. Don't try and reinvent the wheel. Save money, time and aggravation by hiring someone to develop a roadmap for you to succeed with.

Of course, we always take our own advice. In the case of the illustrators, we bring on for our comics, they are artists who currently work with the biggest in the business.

When you've incorporated all seven game changers into your business, you may find that you've not only beaten your competition but that they will also no longer be able to compete with you. This philosophy is displayed in a poignant scene in The

Magnificent Seven where Chris (played by Yul Bryner) and a villager discuss Britt, played by James Coburn.

Villager: If he's the best with the gun and the knife, with whom does he compete?

Chris: Himself.

When you've mastered "The Magnificent Seven" game changers, the only company left to compete with could be your own. Every week, set out to top your best week. The same goes for every month and every year. This is what it means to be the very best at what you do.

Proven Actions to Take:

- Gain the Necessary Visibility That You Need.
- Attain the Necessary Authority and Credibility That You Need.
- Refuse to Limit Yourself in Your Marketing and Advertising Mediums.
- Gain the Necessary Understanding of the Proven Principles of Influence and Persuasion.
- Most Importantly, Gain the Sound Advice of a Proven Professional Who Has Attained the Great Achievements That You Strive For.

Book a No-Charge, No-Obligation Consultation

to Gain the Visibility You Need

to Make your Profits Soar:

https://SmithProfits.com/Contact/

Chapter Nine:
Smile, You're On Branded Camera:
Why Companies Should Include Smiles In Their Branding

Smith Comics Smile Logo

Problems that Businesses Face:

- They Fail to Learn the Power of the Smile from Market Leaders
- They Lack Creativity in Their Logo Design(s)
- They Lack an Understanding of the Principle of Liking
- They Lack an Understanding of the Power of Images

Smith's Forbes Article:

The Internet Movie Database (IMDb) logline for the hit television show Candid Camera is, "Unsuspecting people are placed in confusing, impossible, embarrassing, ridiculous, and hilarious positions, while their reactions are recorded on a hidden camera."

There is no doubt that companies that fail to brand their products and services effectively will also find themselves in "confusing, impossible, embarrassing, ridiculous, and hilarious positions." Brands tell stories. Do you want the story of your business to be a sad one or a happy one? Put a smile on your customers' faces and you'll put a smile on your own face.

My brother, Ron, learned this long ago. In fact, as a painter, he begins every job by painting a smile in a prominent place that eventually gets painted over.

Nevertheless, that's Ron's trademark, and that smile will last as long as each particular building does. Not only that but also Ron provides every customer with what he terms his "All Smiles Guarantee." Ron's smile tells the story of his business. His customers know they can expect to have a happy experience with Ron and his crew members. They know this from referrals and Ron's reputation. They all come together to tell the story of the painting business.

What's your business story? The first part of your story that potential customers see is your company logo. I believe this is why so many successful companies place smiles in their logos. Here are some well-known examples of brands that use imagery representative of smiles:

- Colgate's branding makes the most sense, as it promotes its products as solutions to more beautiful smiles.
- Amazon may be the most famous logo with a smile on it.
- Dannon/Danone gave its health-focused foods a logo boost to help people smile.
- Kraft Mac & Cheese took things a step further and turned a macaroni noodle into a smile.

We were so impressed with the statistics on providing subliminal smiles in branding that we upgraded our RobertJSmith.com, Smith Profits, Robert

J. Smith Productions and Smith Comics logos with upward curves that represent smiles as well.

Lay's took smiles seriously in a campaign called "The Smile Stories" to help make lives better. Here is an excerpt from the Now This website: "Lay's is celebrating people across the country who inspire smiles in their communities in extraordinary ways ... Each Smile with Lay's bag you buy helps us reach our goal of a $1 million donation to Operation Smile – a nonprofit that changes and saves lives one smile at a time."

Operation Smile takes smiles seriously as well. However, smiles are not a for-profit business for Operation Smile as it is for Frito-Lay and Colgate. Operation Smile operates as a not-for-profit 501(c)(3) organization that provides life-improving cleft surgery, dentistry, orthodontics, speech therapy and psychological services. This organization makes me think of a young girl named Veda Roznowski, who this article is dedicated to. She passed away at the tender age of one due to complications from anesthesia at a local hospital during a surgery Operation Smile specializes in.

"Let us always meet each other with a smile, for the smile is the beginning of love," Mother Teresa is known to have said.

The world's largest companies have leveraged

the emotions of happiness and love in their branding and advertising campaigns to elicit feelings of unity which greatly influence our buying decisions.

"Have a Coke and a Smile" is one example. The world's largest soft drink manufacturer had great success with its campaign of togetherness and symmetry, which culminates in the huge success of its Mean Joe Greene Super Bowl ad that featured his fictional meeting with a young fan.

Even the word "smile" can sell without anyone actually seeing a smiling face. Dean Martin, Doris Day and many others sold a massive number of records with the song "Powder Your Face With Sunshine." "Powder your face with sunshine," the lyrics say. "Put on a great big smile. Make up your eyes with laughter. Folks will be laughing with you in a little while. Whistle a tune of gladness. Blue never was in style. The future's brighter when hearts are lighter. So, smile, smile, smile."

Dozens of artists sold records with the song "When You're Smiling," which was first published in 1928. "When you're smiling, when you're smiling, the whole world smiles with you," the lyrics say. "When you're laughing, when you're laughing, the sun comes shining through. But when you're crying, you bring on the rain. So, stop your sighing, be happy again. Keep on smiling, 'cause when you're smiling, the whole world smiles with you."

Of course, Smile was the album the Beach Boys abandoned in 1967. When Brian Wilson resurrected Smile in 2004, he earned his first Grammy with one of its tracks, and Brian Wilson Presents Smile reached No. 13 in the U.S. and No. 7 in the U.K. (paywall). BWPS also landed in Rolling Stone's "500 Greatest Albums Of All Time."

"A smile is the best makeup any girl can wear," Marilyn Monroe is famously attributed with saying.

Here's the best news: Research has shown that you don't even need an obvious, full-blown smile. An upward curve does the trick. We've updated our logos at Smith Profits with upward curves across the board, and we're having a record fourth quarter as a result.

A combined research study in Colombia and the United Kingdom said that "these findings provide both a deeper theoretical understanding of the influence of subtle cues on evaluation and decision making, and concrete, practical information for both product designers and marketers."

Don't fail to brand your company's products and services effectively and find yourself in "confusing, impossible, embarrassing, ridiculous, and hilarious positions." Instead, brand your products and services effectively, and you'll always smile, whether you are on camera or not.

Proven Actions to Take:

- Put the Principle of Liking to Work for You, Just Like America's Leading Companies Do.
- Put the Power of the Smile to Work for You! Use Smiles in Your Logos and Marketing Campaigns.

Book a No-Charge, No-Obligation Consultation to Put the Power of Smiles to Work for You and Your Business:

https://SmithProfits.com/Contact/

Chapter Ten:
'Jingle All The Way' To The Bank:
Why Your Business
Needs A Strong Jingle

Smith Profits Smile Logo

Smith Profits Animated Jingle

https://youtu.be/QyaPHcmU11k

Problems that Businesses Face:

- Their Advertising Lacks Strong Hooks
- Their Products and Services Lack Quality Jingles

Smith's Forbes Article:

The logline for Jingle All the Way, my son Austin's favorite, is, "A father vows to get his son a Turbo Man action figure for Christmas. However, every store is sold out, and he must travel all over town and compete with everybody else in order to find one."

In this holiday movie, Arnold Schwarzenegger plays mattress salesman Howard Langston, whose tagline is "You're my No. 1 customer." Howard competes like all parents who ever had a child who wanted something when that gift was in short supply.

Even with a comical tagline, Howard competed in business as fiercely as he competed with Christmas shoppers. Are your taglines up to snuff? Do they help you compete? How about a jingle? Have you created a jingle for your business?

My company creates custom jingles for businesses, and I've found that they are a cost-effective method of marketing and advertising. They help cement your brand in the minds of potential customers. Jingles are attention-grabbing devices that help your company stand apart from the competition. When done right, jingles help you stand head and shoulders above the competition. They become a major brand element that are as important as your company logo. The best jingles are memorable. They enhance brand recall, improve customer acquisition, and enhance customer loyalty.

While I've won awards for the art of storytelling as well as editing for film, games and animation, I left the writing of our first jingle to a specialist for two reasons:

1. He has written numerous successful jingles and I haven't.
2. While I can sing, I play a sub standard guitar and nothing else, while he has a professional studio staffed with professional musicians.

The creation of a jingle is a simple process when you work with a professional. An experienced jingle writer should ask you questions about your brand and review your logos as well as any mascots that enhance your brand. A jingle writer will need to know about your target customer and how you intend to incorporate your jingle to enhance your brand.

If you haven't created an official jingle, use some of America's most recognized for inspiration.

- Alka Seltzer: "Plop, plop. Fizz, fizz. Oh, what a relief it is!" In one of the most memorable commercials in the history of television, we see a husband who isn't feeling well. "I can't believe I ate that whole thing." His unsympathetic wife responds, "You ate it, Ralph."
- •Band-Aid: "I am stuck on Band-Aid brand." Kids somehow make it seem fun to have to stop the bleeding.
- Chilis: "I want my baby back ribs." This jingle was so successful that it was revisited in the film Austin Powers: The Spy Who Shagged Me.
- Coca-Cola: "I'd like to buy the world a Coke." This may be one of the most iconic of all jingles. This short song had such an impact on the American consciousness that it was highlighted in the final episode of the hit television show Mad Men. I'll kick 2024 off with a series of articles here based on individual episodes of that ground-breaking series.
- Klondike: "What would you do for a Klondike bar?" Me? I'd write an article on how effective jingles are. Where is my Klondike bar?
- Nationwide: "Nationwide is on your side." Irma Thomas and The Rolling Stones reminded

us that "time is on [our] side." It's good to know that Nationwide is also on our side.

- Oscar Mayer Wieners: "Oh, I'd love to be an Oscar Mayer wiener!" On a personal note, I brought my children, Ashley, Austin and Sabrina, to the Greenfield Village and Henry Ford Museum on a trip to metro Detroit. I took pictures of all three children in front of the iconic Wienermobile. We even left the museum with Oscar Mayer Wiener whistles. I'll share more on brand merchandising in later articles.
- Slinky: "It's Slinky! It's Slinky!" When you heard "It's fun. It's a wonderful thing" as a child, didn't you want to have one? I did.

Jingles resonate with customers as they create emotional connections. This is important for the simple reason that many people predominately buy with emotion and not with logic. Strong jingles will build brand affinity and create strong customer loyalty that can endure throughout the life of your customer. The strongest of jingles can become generational as parents who patronize your business will have children and grandchildren who will also be likely to patronize your business.

If you haven't created a jingle, your business is missing out on one of the most cost-effective methods of marketing and advertising to acquire customers and build brand loyalty. If you have created a jingle that isn't performing, it's time for a new one.

Successful jingles aren't much different than successful songs. You never know where your inspiration will come from. As Tommy James said about his No. 1 smash hit "Mony Mony," "We got out on my terrace and the first thing our eyes fall on was the Mutual of New York building. M.O.N.Y. with the dollar sign in the middle of the 'O.' It would give you the time and the weather. We just started laughing because it hit us both at the same time. That was the perfect name for the song." There is my connection with Tommy. He had a No. 1 hit with "Mony Mony" in the U.K., Billy Idol hit No. 1 in the U.S. with it, and I was No. 1 worldwide with MONY.

The most essential element in both jingles and hit songs is the hook. Here is ours:

"... When your bottom line's not pretty,

count on Smitty

to hammer out profits for your business ..."

Keep it short. Keep it catchy. Keep it profitable.

Create a memorable jingle and unlike Arnold Schwarzenegger's Howard Langston, you'll be able to dominate your competition. When your jingle resonates with customers, you'll "jingle all the way" to the bank.

Proven Actions to Take:

- Build Strong Hooks into Your Marketing and Advertising
- Have a Professional Team Create Quality Jingles for Your Products and Services

Book a No-Charge, No-Obligation Consultation

to Create Your Professionally Produced

Profit-Earning Jingle:

https://SmithProfits.com/Contact/

Chapter Eleven: 'Friendly Persuasion': The Psychology Of Influence

FRIENDLY PERSUASION Movie Poster 1948

Problems that Businesses Face:

- They fail to understand and leverage the proven principles of influence and persuasion to drive sales, revenues, and profits.

Smith's Forbes Article:

The best tag line for the film Friendly Persuasion, which featured Gary Cooper, Dorothy McGuire and Anthony Perkins as the Birdwells, a family of pacifists drawn into the American Civil War, was, "Try FRIENDLY PERSUASION: It's Powerful!" I was so impressed with this movie promotion that I tried it.

Within six months of reading Influence, the Psychology of Persuasion by Robert Cialdini, Ph.D., I was ranked No. 1 in worldwide production with MONY/AXA Equitable. (Full disclosure: I'm a founding member of the Cialdini Institute.) It wasn't the reading alone that created that success; it was putting the good doctor's research into action that brought the desired results.

Several decades of evidence-based research went into Influence, which sold more than 5 million copies worldwide. In that seminal work, there were six principles of influence: reciprocity, scarcity, authority, consistency, liking and social proof. A subsequent release added a seventh principle of influence, unity.

Here's how I've made these proven principles work for maximum client acquisition and sales over the past three decades:

Authority

As Will Rogers purportedly said, "You never get a second chance to make a first impression." Most often, a prospective client's first impression of you and your business will come from your website. Be sure to include all major network television logos and other media brands on your website to denote coverage and add necessary credibility.

Make sure, as I have always done, that your biography includes all of your academic credentials and professional designations, such as BBA, MBA, MFA, Ph.D., RIA, CLU, CHFC, LIC, AAMS, etc.

If your website is set up correctly and it's done its job, your prospect will book an initial consultation through your site. You're on your way to the next step.

Reciprocity

Prior to your discovery interview or first appointment, provide your prospect with a gift of value. Only a gift of proven value will work to invoke this principle. For example, we first provide prospects with a digital copy of Influence.

To stay in the top 1% of worldwide financial services ranking, we used to mail out hard copies of the comic I wrote about a superhero insurance agent who explained complex topics in an easy-to-understand manner. Hard copies have been known to have a shelf life of years, and I've found they also tend to get passed on to other potential clients. We've never found or created a better tool for obtaining referrals.

These are upfront gifts of value that use sales psychology to increase client acquisition and sales through storytelling and research-based evidence. These gifts invoke a social obligation to return the favor by making prospects and clients more likely to buy and invest as well as to refer new business.

Always attach a welcome letter to your gift in order to set expectations for your initial and subsequent appointments. Your welcome letter should include content with two or three of these essential elements of persuasion.

Scarcity

Key points to get across: I can only meet with so many people in a year. Each prospective client gets only one shot to do business with me. I'm far too busy for second chances. I am in demand, and my time is limited. It's a simple truth. This truth is confirmed by my calendar, which is posted on our primary website, and you can do the same by sharing your availability on your own website. Avoid any trendy and overused false scarcity tactics such as "limited time" and "this offer ends ... never to return." Sophisticated buyers see through such tired and blatantly false tactics.

Consistency

Include examples of generational clients. Gain coverage on multiple television networks, newspapers, magazines and even podcast streaming services. Display this coverage on your websites, in email signatures and on other marketing pieces to improve closing ratios in discovery and subsequent interviews.

Liking

Clients repeatedly refer to businesses and advisors they like and trust. This also sets the stage that referrals are earned and expected. Tell clients stories of other clients who have referred you and how well you made those clients look at work, their country club, in their neighborhood, etc.

Social Proof

Gain celebrity and/or industry endorsements as evidence that you are a trusted source and a go-to person in your industry. For example, on our landing page, we include an endorsement from an original Shark from Shark Tank. There is no better authority than a referral from a satisfied client. Qualified referrals should be closed 100% of the time.

In addition to using media sources that provide

instant social proof, use client success stories. For example: "We saved a Massachusetts picture framing company over $65,000 in annual business taxes after discovering a deduction that their CPA missed for 20 years running."

Unity

Work with affinity groups of clients such as medical societies, school districts, professional athletes, etc.

All of this preparation upfront fully prepares prospects to freely accept your message before you deliver it to them. Their defenses are down, and you have placed yourself in an optimal position to gain them as a new client. It then becomes your primary focus to service them to the best of your ability so that you earn maximum referrals from them. Every time you hit a home run for them, ask them who they know who can benefit from similar successes.

We may not be of the Friendly Persuasion, and we hope to never have to battle through another American Civil War like the Birdwell family did. However, we can all rest assured that the art of friendly and ethical persuasion can help you reach new heights in your business and in your industry as it did for me.

Proven Actions to Take:

- Learn Everything You Need to Know, in Order

to Leverage the Proven Principles of Influence and Persuasion to Drive Sales, Revenues, and Profits.

Book a No-Charge, No-Obligation Consultation to Gain Access to Everything You Need to Succeed Through the Ethical Use of Influence and Persuasion:

https://SmithProfits.com/Contact/

Chapter Twelve:
'Mad Men':
Learning From the Greats to Influence Buyers

Plaque in the Lobby of the

Iconic New York Life Building

51 Madison Avenue, New York, NY

Courtesy New York Life Insurance Company

Problems that Businesses Face:

- They lack an understanding of proven business strategies that stand the test of time.
- They fail to follow the lead of corporate giants.

Smith's Forbes Article:

Here is the logline for the hit television show Mad Men, according to IMDb: "A drama about one of New York's most prestigious ad agencies at the beginning of the 1960s, focusing on one of the firm's most mysterious but extremely talented ad executives, Donald Draper."

While I don't consider myself to be a "Mad Man," I am fortunate enough to have my name on a plaque in the lobby of the New York Life Building on Madison Avenue, along with a great team of agents who comprised the group that helped the insurance giant lead the Million Dollar Round Table for the 50th consecutive year.

While New York Life is in the Fortune 100 and can afford to work with any advertising agency that it chooses, most of us do not enjoy the same luxury. I've had to create my own marketing and advertising over the past five decades. "I have stood on the shoulders of giants," as Isaac Newton famously said.

I began by studying greats such as John Caples, David Ogilvy and, most recently, George Lois. I was fortunate enough to speak with the latter legendary "Mad Man" before he passed away. I called Lois after reading his book Damn Good Advice (for People with Talent!): How to Unleash Your Creative Potential by America's Master Communicator.

In a 2012 CNN article, Lois wrote, "'Mad Men' is nothing more than the fulfillment of every possible stereotype of the early 1960s." He also said, "Unlike the TV 'Mad Men,' we worked full, exhausting, joyous days."

Make your days less exhausting and a lot more joyous by following systems that have already been researched and tested for you. That's what I've done from the start of my career. I discovered the work of famed American engineer and statistician W. Edwards Deming. I've always made efforts to create efficient and repeatable systems for everything we do. As the man said, "A system must create something of value, in other words, results."

I created my very first advertisement in 1993. It read: "BILL CLINTON'S NEW BUDGET PLAN CALLS FOR THE LARGEST TAX INCREASE IN WORLD HISTORY! FREE Report Reveals 10 Secrets to Keeping His Hands Out of Your Pockets! Call 1-800-707-6514 24 Hrs., for a Free Recorded Message to Find Out How You Can Beat the New Tax Increase!"

The result of my inaugural $500 print ad? I

received 306 leads overnight. Within 24 hours of the release in a small, suburban Detroit newspaper, I had a flood of leads looking for my solutions. The resulting clients kept me so busy, I never ran another ad that year.

I had created an effective system for creating leads and appointments. While John Hancock had no extraordinary training systems, I was able to learn quite a lot from my general agent who was kind enough to share his decades of successful experience with me. One of the most important things I learned from him early on was when I was struggling to compete against veteran advisors from other companies to attract business from the Big Three automakers.

With limited experience at the age of 25 and a young family to feed, I found myself in advanced markets slugging it out with veteran advisors with master's degrees and connections. My general agent deftly pointed out to me that I lacked authority and that this could be gained through earning the Chartered Life Underwriter (CLU) and Chartered Financial Consultant (ChFC) designations through The American College. The trouble was that I didn't want to wait multiple years to complete the 13 required programs necessary to earn them. So, I got to work and cranked them out in only 13 months while working full time at the agency. To my knowledge, that had never before been accomplished at the legendary company and hasn't been since.

A decade later, I found myself in the middle of the Mutual of New York (MONY)/AXA Equitable merger and trying to blend the systems of three different companies. It was at that time I had the good fortune of having another Million Dollar Round Table member recommend a book to me. That book was Influence, the Psychology of Persuasion written by Robert Cialdini, Ph.D., a researcher at Arizona State University.

Influence was the final piece of the puzzle that I had been putting together for the past dozen years. As I explained in a previous Forbes article, Influence contains six principles of influence and persuasion. I included them in all of my marketing and advertising campaigns. This was a game-changer for me. Within months of putting these principles to use, I was the No. 1 ranked producer worldwide in all three companies.

A seventh principle, unity, was subsequently added as additional research over the years proved a great tendency of people to be influenced in and by their affinity groups. These are groups that they are formally involved with, such as universities, unions, work teams, sports teams or informal groups that people identify with, such as liberals or conservatives.

If you don't want to wait even 13 months to establish your authority, here's how we establish it for our clients much faster and how you can do the same: Create news stories and place them with all major television networks and media outlets. We've seen an average sales increase of 51% with this strategy alone. The same goes for reciprocity. Create persuasive comics that you can use as sales and marketing pieces. Our very first offering netted a six-figure life insurance commission from a single sale.

Stand on the shoulders of giants like I did. You may not have direct access to some of them as I did. However, you certainly have access to the work of greats like Lois, Demings and Cialdini. We bring their combined life's work to all of our clients.

Rather than, "See you in the funny papers," I'll leave you with, "See you on Main Street, if not on Madison Avenue!"

Proven Actions to Take:

- Rank Alongside the Giants Whose Shoulders We Have Always Stood On.

Book a No-Charge, No-Obligation Consultation

to Rank Ahead of Giants, Not Just With Them:

https://SmithProfits.com/Contact/

Epilogue

Now that you have seen, "the rest of the story" it is my sincere hope that you fully take advantage of the lessons learned from the combined successes of American companies over hundreds of years.

You've now got everything you need to increase sales, revenues and profits. If you need any assistance from any of our accomplished co-authors, feel free to reach out to each of them, directly.

If you have any difficulty reaching anyone, let me know, and I will contact them for you.

As stated in this prologue, "Here's to you and here's to your continued success!"

Smitty

A Few Words on Giving Back

As soon as your business is flourishing, it's time to give back to our local communities and our great nation. Whether you want to start your own charity, like I did, or you want to continue with those that you've been involved with, it is up to you.

Just remember that there are more ways to give back than just donating money to those in need. It is our obligation, each of us, to mentor America's youth and teach our children and the children of others, how to achieve success.

I've personally volunteered in schools for the past three decades. I started when my own children were in school, I never stopped when they graduated, and I don't plan to stop, anytime soon.

Whether it's our own children, who may or may not want to follow in our footsteps, it is our obligation to help them get off to a great start. We need to teach them how to think independently, how to work, and how to achieve. It's our obligation to help others, as well.

Here are several examples of how to accomplish this for young Americans who need direction and encouragement, especially in these turbulent times:

1. I've volunteered to teach Entrepreneur pitching in middle schools, high schools and colleges.

We've consistently produced state champions who have earned sponsorships and awards, ranging from $2,000.00 to $10,000.00.

2. I also volunteer to teach public speaking to elementary school students, and I've been fortunate to see many young lives improved through the newfound confidence they gain by moving out of their comfort zones. We teach them how to prepare, how to work efficiently, how to conquer their nerves, and ultimately, how to achieve success.
3. Another way to help America's youth is through our Junior Patriots™ nonprofit. While tax-deductible donations are accepted, our primary mission is to encourage patriotism and provide opportunity to our youth.

Nothing is given. Students have to work for their success. Even that work starts with a simple essay. We're always looking for public and private schools and youth organizations to serve.

For those students who are homeschooled or unaffiliated with a participating youth organization, we create anthologies so that every youngster has the ability to participate. You can even set your own children up for success and teach them patriotism and join them in this project that educates them while it brings families together.

https://JuniorPatriots.us

SCAN ME

"To expect people to be good, to be just, to be temperate, etc., without showing them how they should become so, seems like the ineffectual charity mentioned by the apostle, which consisted in saying to the hungry, the cold and the naked, be ye fed, be ye warmed, be ye clothed, without showing them how they should get food, fire or clothing." **-Benjamin Franklin**

"The best thing to give to your enemy is forgiveness; to an opponent, tolerance; to a friend, your heart; to your child, a good example; to a father, deference; to your mother, conduct that will make her proud of you; to yourself, respect; to all others, charity." **-Benjamin Franklin**

Sign your children or grandchildren up

to become Junior Patriots™ and

#1 Best Selling Authors in our series,

WHAT I LOVE ABOUT AMERICA!

Become a #1 Best Selling Author, Yourself

Now, that you've taken care of your family, take care of your business and your legacy.

Become a #1 Best Selling Author in our #1 Best Selling INFLUENCE IN ACTION™ series.

Whether you are a CEO, or a professional with something to offer, feel free to contact me for your own chapter in one of our upcoming books, so that you may become a ***#1 Best Selling Author.*** *You'll immediately be able to increase your credibility and authority to increase your income.* ***The median increase in income for businesspeople with #1 Best Selling Books is $96,000.00 annually!***

If you are a public speaker, you will find yourself to be even more in demand than you already are. You'll not only be able to increase your fees per presentation, as ***the average fee increase nationwide is 350%,*** *you'll also naturally increase the amount of speaking gigs that you are able to book. In addition to that, you'll find that your audience engagement begins to boom, and your sales closing ratios will skyrocket to optimal rates.*

Here is an example: I recently attended a three-day conference that many of my clients attend, here in Orlando. One speaker after another got up onstage and I noticed the same thing, day after day, after day.

When people 2,000 – 3,000 attendees sat down at various ten-top tables, they immediately began talking, drinking coffee and eating pastries. Some immediately got onto their computers, or other electronic devices, oblivious to what was going on around them.

When speakers were introduced, nothing changed. People kept eating, drinking, working, and even worse, they continued talking. All this when they should have been paying attention to the professional onstage.

By comparison, when speakers were introduced as **#1 Best Selling Authors**, everything changed. The food and drinks were immediately set down. Electronic devices were closed, except for attendees taking notes, and everyone sat up straight, to pay attention. Some sat up straight and tall, with pen and notepad in hand.

Each speaker who was introduced as a **#1 Best Selling Author** had 2,000 – 3,000 potential clients engaged and ready to buy. Each of them was surrounded by prospects the minute they walked offstage, as well.

The difference between speakers introduced as ***#1 Best Selling Authors*** *and those who were not, was like night and day. The audience reaction was not only consistent, day after day, I saw the exact same thing happen* *at several conferences, since.*

See if you notice the same thing, the next time you are at a local or national conference. I'll be amazed if you don't.

If you want the same authority and respect that being a ***#1 Best Selling Author*** *provides to you, whether you speak to audiences or not, contact me. You can either write a chapter in our* ***#1 Best Selling Series*** *or you can write your own book. Either way, we will market you to a* ***#1 Best Seller.***

When a prospective customer or client asks you what make you an expert on your industry, you can legitimately say, that you "Wrote the book on it."

SCAN ME

"I have written four books and worked with a couple well known publishers. I was introduced to Robert J. Smith, MFA. He reviewed my most recent book, gave me sound advice and promoted the book and applied marketing at a high level.

Through his work with his team players the book soon became a #1 International Best Seller, which now appears on the cover. He has many services to promote products. I highly recommend him."

-Ron Wallace, Retired President of UPS International

About Your Author

ROBERT J. SMITH, MFA

Born in metro Detroit, Smitty learned to compete at a young age, winning baseball championships in his first season at the age of nine and in his final season at the age of thirty, including a streak of six out of his first eight seasons, all on eight different teams.

His work ethic was developed in his blue-collar beginnings. No one in the history of Automobile Capital of the World, or in the Great State of Michigan, has completed more oil changes in one day, one week, or one month than Smitty has. In fact, he averaged two cars at once from 6:30 a.m. to midnight, seven days per week, for thirty-one straight days during a Mobil Oil recall in the early 1980s.

After moving to Florida, Smitty and another route driver teamed up to complete all of their deliveries after every other route truck driver for Coca-Cola was called back into the warehouse during Hurricane Elena. After developing the #1 home market merchandising route in the Sarasota territory, Smitty suffered an on-the-job injury which led to a career change into the financial services industry.

As a financial services advisor, Smitty reached #1 worldwide rankings at AXA Financial, The Equitable, Mutual of New York (MONY), and BankAtlantic. He set records at John Hancock and New York Life. His name is enshrined in a plaque on Madison Avenue.

https://SmithProfits.com/

SCAN ME

Debilitating spine and other severe injuries necessitated a career change. While undergoing multiple surgeries to regain the ability to walk, he concurrently earned his Master of Fine Arts (MFA) in Creative Writing as Valedictorian at Full Sail University, and his Feature Film Writing degree "With Distinction" at UCLA. He holds Director's Awards for "The Art of Visual Storytelling" as well as for "Editing for Film, Games, and Animation."

https://RobertJSmith.com

Smith's consulting practice helps financial advisors reach the top 1% in worldwide production, entertainers reach the top 1% in the Internet Movie Database (IMDb), and every client gain top Google search rankings.

https://RobertJSmithProductions.com

He is an International Best-Selling Author with ***SALES GENIUS #1***©, which bested The Wolf of Wall Street's book on sales. ***THE ADVENTURES OF INSURANCEMAN***©

increases sales for clients and their companies. Smith created ***SHORT ATTENTION SPAN DAN***© to teach writing and public speaking to students.

https://www.Amazon.com/Author/RobertJSmith

After earning his Leadership Certification in Influencing People at the University of Michigan,

Smith has turned many businesspeople into #1 International Bestselling Authors.

Smith and his companies have been featured on ABC, CBS, CW, FOX, The Golf Channel, NBC, WGN, and hundreds of other media outlets.

https://www.IMDb.Me/RobertJSmith

He's been named to the Entrepreneur Magazine Leadership Network, the Inc. Leadership Forum, the Fast Company Executive Board, and the Forbes Business Council.

https://www.Forbes.com/Councils/ForbesBusinessCouncil/People/SmittyRobertJSmith/

Smith's other books are available at fine booksellers everywhere, as well as:

https://SmithBusinessBooks.com

Smith raised millions for charity and volunteers in public and private schools. Within 24-hours in 2024, one of his high school students, and one of his medical school students each won their Entrepreneur Pitch Championships and earned sizable cash prizes to develop each of their medical products that will greatly benefit mankind.

He's served as a Field Councilman for the Greater Detroit Area Life Underwriters, Board Member of the Tampa Bay United Way, Treasurer of World League Baseball, and President of the Executive Sports Council. Smith currently serves as President of the Junior Patriots™ Corp.

He lives in Winter Garden, Florida, with Sharon Roznowski and has three grown children: Ashley, Austin, and Sabrina.

INFLUENCE IN ACTION™

Your Key to Success!

https://InfluenceInActionBooks.com/

Scan Me!

Coming Soon

INFLUENCE IN ACTION™

for LEGAL PROFESSIONALS©

INFLUENCE IN ACTION™

to EDUCATE STUDENTS©

INFLUENCE IN ACTION™

for AUTOMOTIVE PROFESSIONALS©

INFLUENCE IN ACTION™

for REAL ESTATE PROFESSIONALS©

And, our most ambitious project to-date:

WHAT I LOVE ABOUT AMERICA! ©

A revolutionary new book series where we will help thousands of students and teachers, plus administrative and support staff to become

#1 Best Selling Authors!

Our goal is to encourage American patriotism in 250 public and private schools and youth organizations to celebrate our nations' 250th anniversary.

To become involved and support this project,

please feel free to reach out to me direct at

(407) 508-0200 and/or

Robert@RobertJSmith.com

Thank you.

SCAN ME

https://JuniorPatriots.us

Coming Soon from SMITH COMICS™:

ISSUE #1 in our JUNIOR PATRIOTS™ series,

WASHINGTON'S ONE-MAN ARMY©

Upcoming JUNIOR PATRIOTS™ Titles:

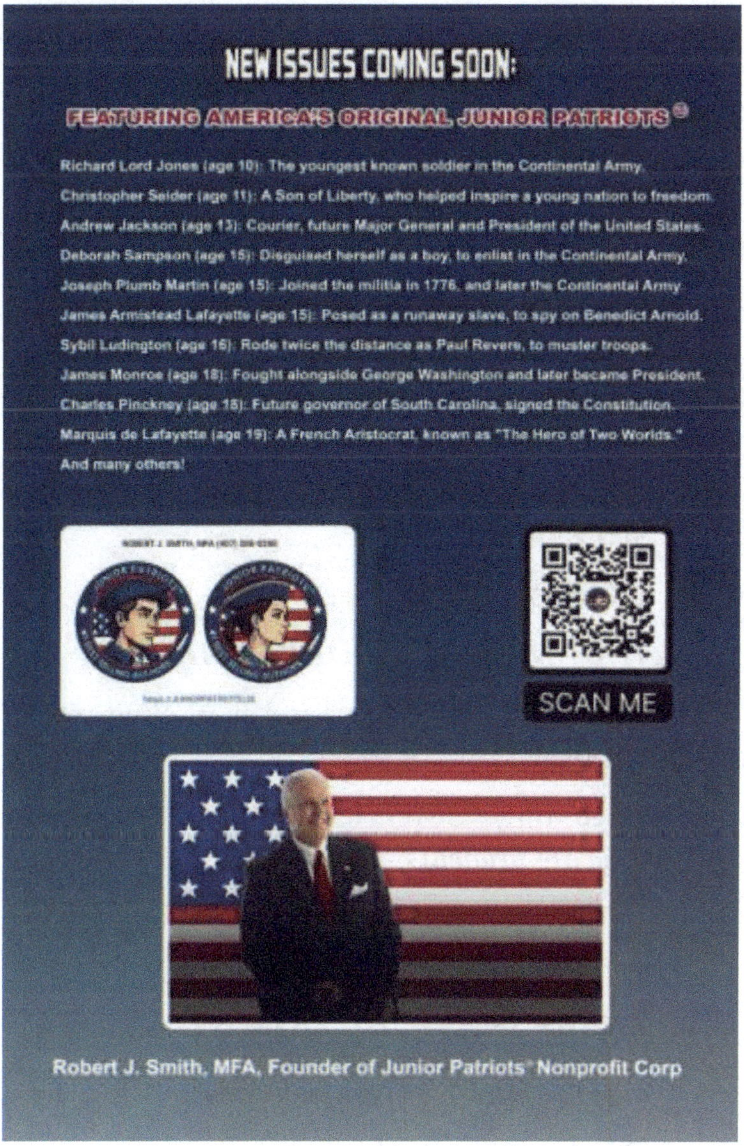

Upcoming SMITH COMICS™ Titles

for You to Use in Sales and Marketing,

to Increase Sales, Revenues and Profits:

THE ADVENTURES OF INSURANCEWOMAN©

REAL ESTATE WOMAN©

REAL ESTATE MAN©

THE AMAZING WEBSITE-MAN©

THE LOAN ARRANGER©

SUPER DENTIST©

SHERRY MASON©

THE ADVENTURES OF BERNIE BURNS©

And any custom sales and marketing piece to suit your business.

Upcoming SMITH COMICS™ Titles *to Educate Students*

SHORT ATTENTION SPAN DAN:

THE GREAT HOUDAN©

SHORT ATTENTION SPAN DAN:

WILD THING, YOU MOVE ME©

Current titles may be found here:

https://www.Amazon.com/Author/RobertJSmith

SMITH COMICS™

Book your no cost, initial consultation now at:

https://SmithProfits.com/Contact

SCAN ME

Learn how you can eliminate your business problems and optimize all of your opportunities:

https://SmithProfits.com

SMITH PROFITS™

TM

SMITHPROFITS.COM

WE'LL HAMMER OUT PROFITS FOR YOUR BUSINESS

#1 BEST SELLERS from SMITH BUSINESS BOOKS™:

https://SmithBusinessBooks.com

https://SmithBusinessBooks.com

https://SmithBusinessBooks.com

https://SmithBusinessBooks.com

"Applause waits on success."

-Benjamin Franklin

Book a no-charge, no-obligation consultation at:

https://SmithProfits.com/Contact/

SCAN ME

Made in the USA
Monee, IL
03 November 2026

67387590R00079